ULTIMATE FANTASY ART

Gothic Horror

PowerKiDS press

JUAN CALLE AND WILLIAM POTTER

Published in 2020 by **The Rosen Publishing Group, Inc.**
29 East 21st Street, New York, NY 10010

Cataloging-in-Publication Data

Names: Calle, Juan. | Potter, William.
Title: Gothic horror / Juan Calle and William Potter.
Description: New York : PowerKids Press, 2020. | Series: Ultimate fantasy art | Includes glossary
and index.
Identifiers: ISBN 9781725303188 (pbk.) | ISBN 9781725303201 (library bound) |
ISBN 9781725303195 (6pack)
Subjects: LCSH: Horror in art--Juvenile literature. | Fantasy in art--Juvenile literature. |
Drawing--Technique--Juvenile literature.
Classification: LCC N8217.H68 C355 2020 | DDC 741.2--dc23

Manufactured in the United States of America

CPSIA Compliance Information: Batch CSPK19: For Further Information contact Rosen Publishing,
New York, New York at 1-800-237-9932.

CONTENTS

FANTASY COMES TO LIFE!

Welcome to the world of fantasy! From vampire lords to fiendish werewolves, there is lots of Gothic horror to create in this book.

All you need to get started is a pencil and paper, but here are a few more tools you can use to add some extra magic.

Pencils come in various hardnesses—H for hard, B for soft. A 2H pencil is good for making light marks that don't smudge, and 2B for adding softer finishes for feathers, fur, and smoke. Try different hardnesses to find those you're most comfortable with. You'll also need a sharpener and eraser.

Collect pictures to inspire you. Models and figurines are also useful as reference for drawing your own fantasy folk.

Any paper will do for drawing on, especially for early sketches and planning. If you use water-based paints, you may want to use a thicker paper that absorbs the paint without it spreading—or bleeding—across the surface.

You can use a waterproof ink pen to go over your pencil lines before painting. Alternatively, use a nib pen or a fine brush dipped in ink. Using a brush and ink requires some patience and a steady hand but can produce impressive results.

For the finished picture use a range of brushes with water-based or acrylic paints, plus a tray or plate to mix different shades.

While many fantasy lands are full of forests, craggy mountains, and crumbling ruins, you may still need to use a ruler as a guide for straight weapons, buildings, mechanical devices, and planning the perspective of an action scene.

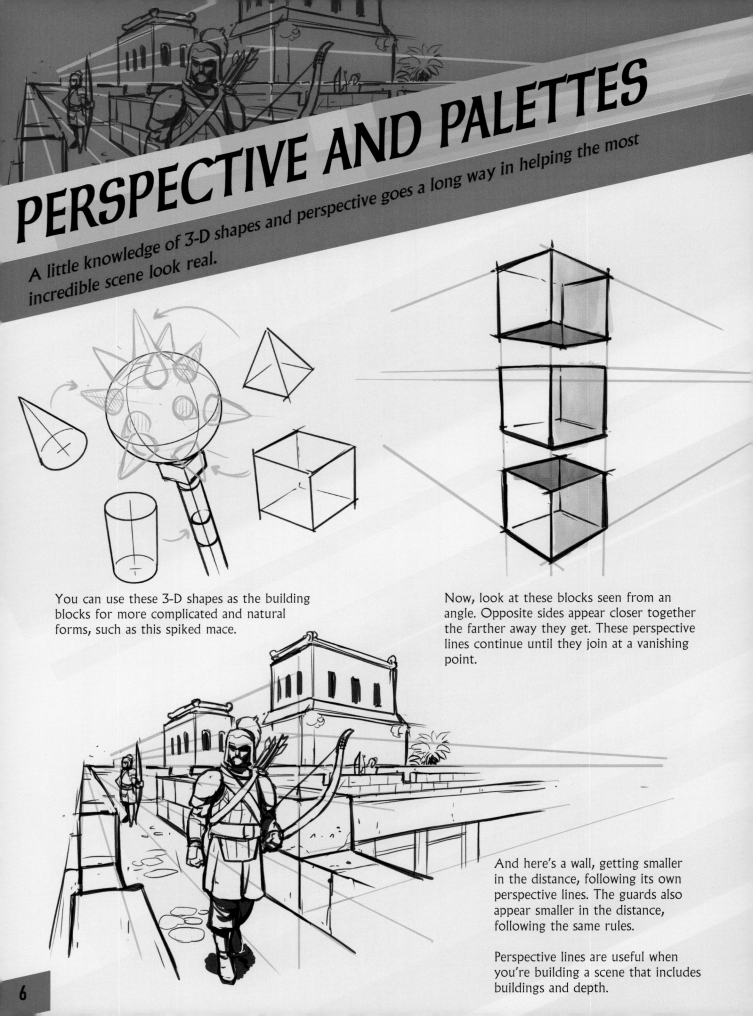

PERSPECTIVE AND PALETTES

A little knowledge of 3-D shapes and perspective goes a long way in helping the most incredible scene look real.

You can use these 3-D shapes as the building blocks for more complicated and natural forms, such as this spiked mace.

Now, look at these blocks seen from an angle. Opposite sides appear closer together the farther away they get. These perspective lines continue until they join at a vanishing point.

And here's a wall, getting smaller in the distance, following its own perspective lines. The guards also appear smaller in the distance, following the same rules.

Perspective lines are useful when you're building a scene that includes buildings and depth.

Reds suggest blood, fire, and passion. Use these to raise the temperature of your fantasy scenes, when dragons use their flaming breath or demons arise from dark domains.

Browns and greens are calming, reminding you of nature. Many adventures involve quests across countrysides. Create drama by beginning a journey in a relaxing green environment and transitioning to a more threatening domain of red and black.

Blues are cooler. They suggest frosty, unfeeling, ghostly moods. Use these for moonlit scenes and the chilly castles of vampires.

HORROR SHOW

A moonlit night, a remote village, church ruins, a dense forest—we're in the territory of Gothic horror, a world of vampires and werewolves—and those brave enough to face them!

HANDSOME VAMPIRE

Vampires appear in many guises. Will you design a ghoul or a charmer? This vampire may look young, but he is hundreds of years old, kept youthful thanks to his vampire curse. He can only leave his secret lair after dark, search for his prey, and drink their blood. His victims then share his curse, building into an army of vampires.

VAMPIRE STYLE

Unable to face the daylight, the vampire has pearly white skin. His hypnotic eyes are green and piercing—one look could entrap you. He carries a cane and wears clothes from another age. The vampire's smile reveals fangs, and the blood he wipes from his lips is a sign he has just feasted.

WEREWOMAN

Who will you choose to bear the burden of the werewolf's curse? Every month, as the full moon rises, this unfortunate woman goes through a painful transformation, becoming wolflike and hungry for flesh.

WEREWOMAN STYLE

The crescent-moon pendant and ragged clothing are clues that this creature was human before her back arched, her limbs stretched, her jaws extended, and she became a savage wolf creature. Thick fur sprouted from her skin and sharp fangs from her gums. Her eyes show no sign of humanity, only a lust for blood.

A MAN POSSESSED

Dabbling with magic often results in unforeseen circumstances and the release of dark forces. This young man fears losing control, as an evil spirit fights to take him over. His eyes and his palms glow with an infernal flame. The more he dares use his new inhuman powers, the more he is pulled toward the dark.

POSSESSED STYLE

The flames of some dark domain are lighting this man from within. He struggles to hide and control them. His dark clothes match his interest in black magic, but his expression shows fear of what he may have unleashed.

MONSTER HUNTER

Create a tragic background for your heroes and a good reason for them to seek out danger. Having lost her family to a beast of the night, this young woman has trained herself to hunt fiendish creatures. Armed and alert, she follows a trail of blood through the dark.

MONSTER HUNTER STYLE

Having faced many nightmares, this stalker of the supernatural shows no fear. She has researched what weapons are needed to destroy vampires and werewolves. Her crossbow fires arrows cut from sacred wood, and her bandolier holds silver stakes. She wears a selection of charms to ward off attacks.

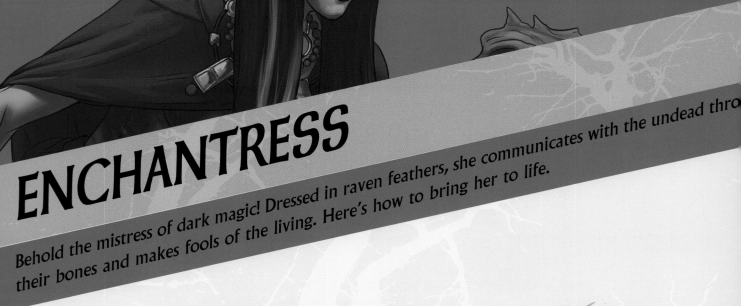

ENCHANTRESS

Behold the mistress of dark magic! Dressed in raven feathers, she communicates with the undead thro[...] their bones and makes fools of the living. Here's how to bring her to life.

1. STICK FIGURE

Using light pencil marks, draw a few simple lines to mark the position of the Gothic witch as she leans forward to talk to the skull in her left hand. A line indicates a curved blade in her right hand.

2. JOINTED FIGURE

Now, fill out her figure with basic 3-D shapes. She has a carefully balanced, slim body. Draw circles to position her joints.

TOP TIP

Here are skulls you can add to your Gothic fantasy scenes. One is human, with a section cut away. The second belongs to a horse. The third is a mix of human and monster, with horns and tusks. These could be ornaments or vessels for communicating with the dead.

3. ANATOMY

Now sketch the enchantress's hair and headdress. Outline the gown over her lower body, with major folds and the beginnings of her skirt of raven feathers.

4. FINISHED PENCILS

Add her facial features, snake wristbands, and detail to her clothes and crown. The skull has a bony crest and fangs. It could not belong to a human.

5. PALETTE

Paint the enchantress in violets and lavenders. Her eyes have a thick line of black around them, and her pale skin has only a hint of pink. Contrast this with her blue eyes and purple lips.

6. FINAL ART

The finished painting uses a lot of dark shades, adding an air of gloom to the character. Blue-black highlights pick out the feathers, and pale reflections have been added to her twisting armbands, headdress, and necklace.

LORD OF THE VAMPIRES

Ruling a nation of bloodsuckers, the lord of the vampires sits on his throne waiting to receive his generals and plan domination of the night.

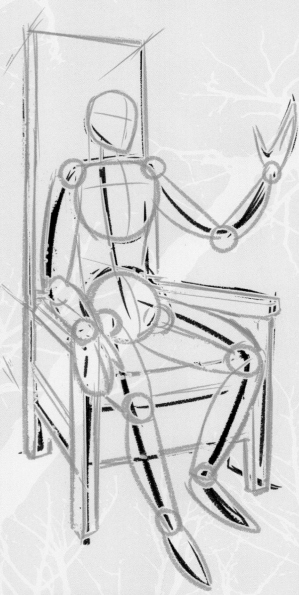

1. STICK FIGURE

Using a few simple lines, mark the seated position of the vampire lord, waving his left hand to greet guests. You may need to use perspective lines to work out the angle of his great throne. The chair's arms are positioned at different angles because of perspective.

2. JOINTED FIGURE

Build up his figure and tall chair with 3-D shapes. Use circles to mark the position of his shoulder, arm, and leg joints.

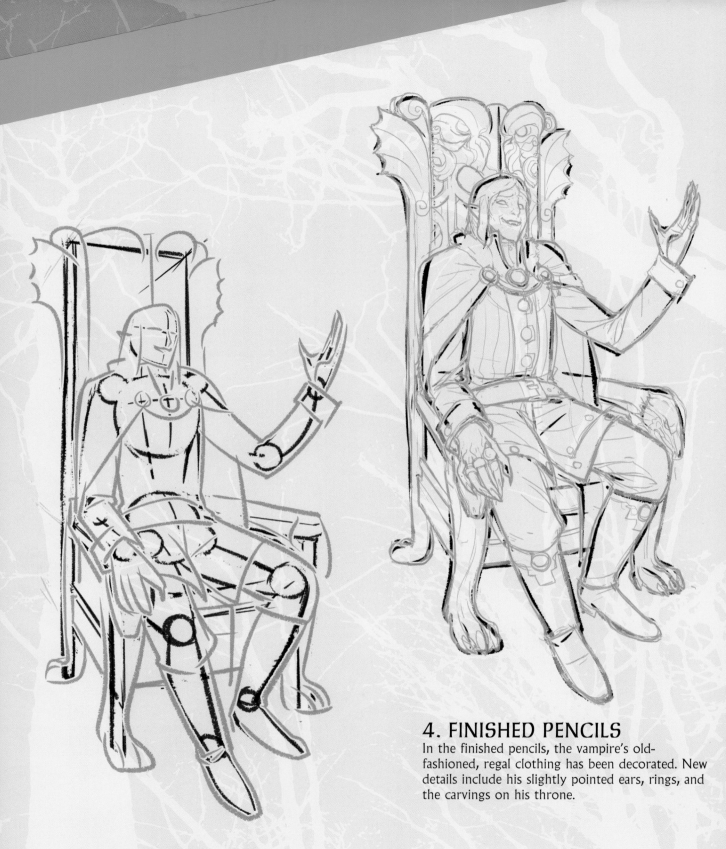

4. FINISHED PENCILS
In the finished pencils, the vampire's old-fashioned, regal clothing has been decorated. New details include his slightly pointed ears, rings, and the carvings on his throne.

3. ANATOMY
Now, refine the lord's figure, with flowing hair, clothing, and the long fingers on his right hand gripping the throne's arm. Add some flourishes on the top and the legs of the grand chair.

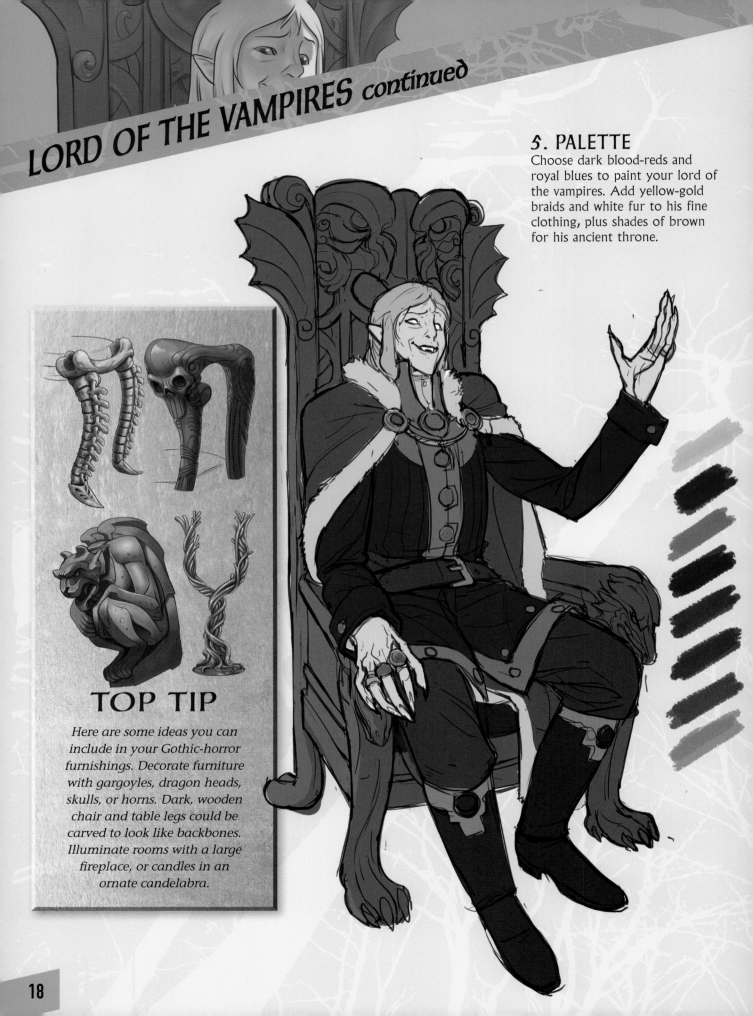

5. PALETTE

Choose dark blood-reds and royal blues to paint your lord of the vampires. Add yellow-gold braids and white fur to his fine clothing, plus shades of brown for his ancient throne.

TOP TIP

Here are some ideas you can include in your Gothic-horror furnishings. Decorate furniture with gargoyles, dragon heads, skulls, or horns. Dark, wooden chair and table legs could be carved to look like backbones. Illuminate rooms with a large fireplace, or candles in an ornate candelabra.

6. FINAL ART

In the finished painting, the lord looks at his finest, in rich velvets and fur trims. His skin is deathly white, lit by a cold blue and pink light. The blood-red in the lord's eyes, his pointed ears, and the hint of fangs remind you he is a vampire.

TRANSFORMATION

From man to wolf—here's how to draw a cursed human turning into a fierce werewolf, one step at a time.

CURSED HUMAN

Under the light of the full moon, the ill-fated man feels a change about to come. He cringes, as he knows the transformation is painful.

TOOTH AND CLAW

His body hunches over as his upper back grows and splits his shirt. His eyes are yellow. His hands have become clawed and his feet are stretching to become more dog-like.

FURRY FIEND

Fur is sprouting all over his body, with thicker hair across the head and shoulders. The head is that of a wild dog with fangs growing. His fingers and toes are now much longer, with pads on the palms.

THE ANIMAL

The transformation is complete. He is now all werewolf, without a trace of humanity. The paws are huge, with long, sharp claws, and thick fur covers his entire body. The hunt is on!

ANIMAL FAMILIARS

Many horror characters are part animal or communicate with wild creatures. Here are some familiars you could use to mingle with your fantasy folk.

RAVEN

The Norse god Odin had a pair of ravens act as his eyes on the world, so you could use this bird as a messenger or a spy. But this clever bird is also said to bring ill fortune or even death. Its dark feathers are glossy, its eyes bright and inquisitive.

TOAD

More than a companion, the toad has been included as an ingredient in witches' brews. As well, many cruel spells have transformed heroes into this warty creature. The toad has a wide mouth, raised eyes, a rounded body, and hind legs with two joints.

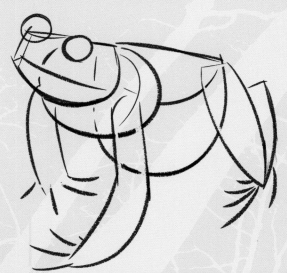

CAT

Traditionally a witch's familiar, the cat is said to add to one's magical powers and have nine lives. It senses evil presences in a room. When prowling, the cat lowers itself to the ground and takes careful, silent steps.

OWL

Owls are thought to represent wisdom. The sound of their hooting at night chills the bones and adds a haunted air to the woods. Sketch a perched owl, beginning with a long oval body and circular head, with wide-open eyes on either side of a triangular brow.

UNDER THE MOONLIGHT

Make your horror scenes appear extra chilling by giving them dramatic lighting.

With a full moon lighting the gravestone from above and to the side, the figure of the angel is mostly in shadow, with bright highlights where the moonlight hits its form. The slow-moving shadows almost bring the mourning angel to life.

The reflected light from the moon casts a silvery blue shade over the ancient mansion. Reds turn to purple shades and greens turn turquoise. One orange light in the building suggests a room is occupied. But, by whom?

24

GATEWAYS

Gateways play a huge part in fantasy adventures. They may hide secret pathways, dark domains, treasure, or prisoners. Often a spell or secret knowledge will be needed to unlock the doors. Here are some examples to inspire your tales.

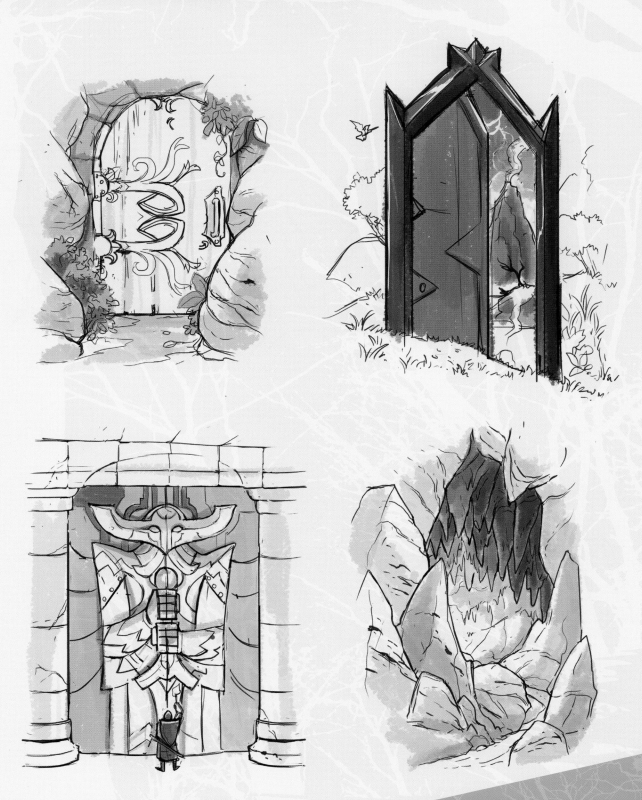

THE UNDEAD RISE

The cemetery is haunted! Our protagonists—a vampire and an enchantress—are being surrounded by the spirits of the dead. Follow the steps to draw the spine-chilling scene.

1. Roughly sketch the scene in miniature, with the two figures encircled by spirits rising from the gravestones and the arch of an ancient tree above.

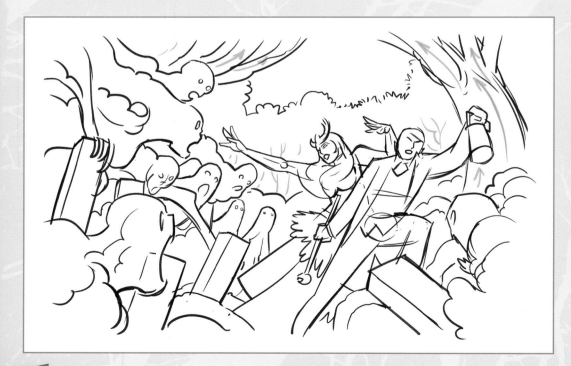

2. Now, start on the full-size drawing, building the two main figures reaching to the left and right. The cloudy spirits only have their upper halves. The gravestones are at different angles, as they have toppled over with age.

3. In these finished pencils, areas of different shading are indicated. The vampire and enchantress stand at dramatic angles in front of a dark background, trying to hold back the rising spirits with spells and lantern light. The spirits have their own unearthly light.

4. The scene is lit by moonlight, so most of the scene is painted with cool, bluish hues. The lantern light is yellow and illuminates the young vampire, bringing out the colors of his clothing.

THE UNDEAD RISE continued

In the final picture, the spirits are painted with bubbling patterns. They rise from the graves like ocean waves. Only the unlikely heroes can make it beyond this dark tide.

GLOSSARY

3-D Three-dimensional, which means having length, breadth, and depth.

anatomy The human body.

bandolier A belt worn over the shoulder and chest, often used to carry ammunition.

black magic Magic that has to do with the devil or evil spirits.

curse A prayer or instruction for harm to come to someone.

enchantress A witch or sorceress.

gargoyles Ugly, carved figures.

Gothic Medieval, or to do with the Middle Ages.

highlight The white area that helps to make a drawing look solid and draw attention to its shape.

humanity The state of being humane, sympathetic, and compassionate.

mace A heavy club used as a weapon.

palette The range of shades chosen by an artist.

perspective The representation on a flat surface of a three-dimensional image as seen by the eye, to give the illusion of distance and depth.

protagonists The main characters in a story.

raven A large bird with glossy black feathers, associated with bad luck.

regal To do with a king or queen.

supernatural Belonging to an existence outside the visible world.

transformation The process of changing from one state to another.

vampire A mythical person believed to come back from the dead to drink the blood of people while they are asleep.

vanishing point The point at which parallel lines seem to meet in the distance.

werewolf A person who can change into a wolf.

FURTHER INFORMATION

Books

Alexander, Rob, and Finlay Cowan and Kevin Walker. *The Compendium of Fantasy Art Techniques*. Hauppauge, NY: Barron's, 2014.

Blando, Jared. *How to Draw Fantasy Art and RPG Maps*. Cincinnati, OH: Impact Books, 2015.

Cook, Trevor, and Lisa Miles. *Drawing Fantasy Figures*. New York, NY: Gareth Stevens Publishing, 2011.

Websites

Art for Kids Hub

www.artforkidshub.com/how-to-draw

This website has instructions for drawing all sorts of things.

How to Draw a Vampire

easydrawingguides.com/how-to-draw-vampire

This page has more information about vampires, as well as step-by-step instructions and a video tutorial on how to draw one!

Publisher's note to educators and parents: Our editors have carefully reviewed these websites to ensure that they are suitable for students. Many websites change frequently, however, and we cannot guarantee that a site's future contents will continue to meet our high standards of quality and educational value. Be advised that students should be closely supervised whenever they access the Internet.

INDEX